Introducing the Sermon

Introducing the Sermon

The Art of Compelling Beginnings

MICHAEL J. HOSTETLER

Zondervan Publishing House • Grand Rapids, MI

INTRODUCING THE SERMON
Copyright © 1986 by Michael J. Hostetler

MINISTRY RESOURCES LIBRARY
is an imprint of
Zondervan Publishing House
1415 Lake Drive S.E.
Grand Rapids, Michigan 49506

Library of Congress Cataloging in Publication Data

Hostetler, Michael J.
　　Introducing the sermon.

　　(The Craft of Preaching Series)
　　"Ministry resources library."
　　Bibliography: p.
　　1. Preaching.　　I. Title.　　II. Series.
BV4211.2.H68　　　　1986　　　251　　　85–29540

ISBN 0–310–30741–4

All Scripture quotations, unless otherwise noted, are taken from the
Holy Bible: New International Version (North American Edition),
copyright © 1973, 1978, 1984 by the International Bible Society.
Used by permission of Zondervan Bible Publishers.

Designed by Louise Bauer
Edited by Joseph Comanda

Printed in the United States of America

91　92　93 / EP / 11　10　9　8　7

To Linda

"She is worth far more than rubies."

Proverbs 31:10

Contents

1. THE PALM OF YOUR HAND   11

2. MAKE CONTACT   17

3. START WITH THE SECULAR   27

4. SPICE UP THE SECULAR   41

5. MOVE TO THE WORD   49

6. LINK WITH THE SERMON SERIES   59

7. TOUCH HOME   67

8. BUILD A BRIDGE   77

    CONCLUSION   85

    NOTES   87

Acknowledgements

I especially want to extend my appreciation to some of the people who helped make this book possible. Ron Burwell, Dorothy Pittman, and Deborah Borisoff offered invaluable advice and encouragement. I am also deeply grateful for the people at Grace Baptist Church, Mahomet, Illinois, and Calvary Baptist Church, Ossining, New York who have endured my own preaching. We have received the Word together, not as the word of men, but as it actually is, the Word of God, and have witnessed its power in our lives (1 Thessalonians 2:13).

1

The Palm of Your Hand

In his book *Telling the Truth*, Frederick Buechner describes the beginning of the sermon.

> The preacher pulls the little cord that turns on the lectern light and deals out his note cards like a riverboat gambler. The stakes have never been higher. Two minutes from now he may have lost his listeners completely to their own thoughts, but at this moment he has them in the palm of his hand. The silence in the shabby church is deafening because everybody is listening to it. Everybody is listening including himself. Everybody knows the kind of things he has told them before and not told them, but who knows what this time, out of the silence, he will tell them.[1]

Every preacher has experienced the exciting sense of expectancy that surrounds the start of a sermon. Every preacher also knows how quickly the audience can wiggle out of "the palm of his hand." Buechner's two-minute estimate is not far off the mark. For a preacher, the two-minute warning comes at the beginning of the game.

In many ways, the introduction is the most important part of sermon delivery. How many brilliant expositions and moving appeals to repentance have been wasted because the audience was lost in the first few minutes of the message? As the great homiletics professor John Broadus put it, " 'Well begun is half done.' And ill begun is apt to be wholly ruined."[2]

All the preaching texts emphasize the importance of the sermon introduction. Haddon Robinson quips, "There are three types of preachers: those to whom you cannot listen; those to whom you can listen; and those to whom you must listen. During the introduction the congregation usually decides the kind of speaker addressing them that morning."[3]

In typical nineteenth-century style, Broadus wrote: "Men have a natural aversion to abruptness, and delight in a somewhat gradual approach. A building is rarely pleasing in appearance without a porch, or something corresponding to a porch. The shining light of dawn, which shineth more and more till the perfect day, teaches us a lesson. And so any composition or address which has no introduction, is apt to look incomplete."[4]

More recently, John Stott simply says, "An introduction is essential."[5]

In spite of their insistence on the introduction's importance, the major texts devote precious little space to it. Broadus gave 10 pages to the introduction in a 541-page work ; Robinson, 7 pages out of 209; and Stott, 2 out of 351. Clearly, sermon introductions deserve a closer look. Exposition is the preacher's great work, but if the introduction falters, the exposition may never be heard.

Why have an introduction? Do all sermons need one? How long should it be? Should it be written out? What about unconventional introductions? Before we begin a nuts-and-bolts analysis of our topic, we should address these important preliminary questions.

What's the purpose of the introduction? Simply stated, the purpose of the introduction is to capture the audience's attention. But not just any attention-getting technique will do. The style and substance of the introduction must be compatible with the sermon's text and thrust. A series of one-liners might get attention but would probably be inappropriate for a funeral message. Moreover, once captured, the audience's attention must be directed toward the Bible, particularly the Bible's timeless power to meet human needs.

Is an introduction always needed? Generally speaking, Broadus's dictum is accurate: "Even if your subject needs no introduction, your audience does."[6] There are exceptions, however. For weddings, funerals, communion services, and other special occasions, the event itself may constitute a nonverbal introduction of sorts.

Bible lectures need introductions too. Though often passed off as sermons, they are different in both purpose and thrust. The Bible lecture is essentially *educational*. Its primary purpose is to explain the biblical text. The sermon, on the other hand, is essentially *motivational*. It uses the explanation of the text as the basis for a personal or corporate response to God. Bible lectures often have no introductions, but they would be better if they did.

How long should the introduction be? The length of the introduction depends on several factors. The more complicated the sermon or text the longer the introduction. If the text is straightforward or familiar to the audience, less time will be needed. The first sermon in a series will require a slightly longer introduction because a few sentences should be devoted to introducing the series itself. As a rule of thumb, however, the introduction should be about twenty percent of the total sermon. That works out to five minutes (two typewritten pages) for a twenty-five minute message. The sermon conclusion, which is invariably easier to compose than the introduction, especially if application has been emphasized throughout the main body of the message, will be slightly shorter. By far the most effective way of timing the introduction is to write it out. Endless, rambling introductions that infringe on the main body of the sermon are almost always the result of poor planning and failure to write.

Must I write it? Homiletics professors as well as parish

preachers have argued among themselves for years about the relative merits of writing out sermon manuscripts. Whether or not to write is still an open question. What to do with the manuscript once it is written poses yet another issue. Should it be memorized and left in the study, carried into the pulpit and read, or used as the basis for developing an extemporaneous outline? To write or not to write? Every preacher must decide.

This book is based on the premise that writing is the key to homiletical discipline and rhetorical style. James S. Stewart put it this way, "You will be advised, whichever method of delivery you are proposing to adopt, to begin by writing out your sermons fully. During the first ten years of your ministry—and perhaps over a much longer period than that—there is no substitute for this essential discipline. It will safeguard your work against diffuseness, ambiguity, and redundance. It will make for clarity of thought and perspicuity of style."[7]

Nowhere are clear thinking and perspicuous style needed more than in the sermon introduction. The discipline, logic, and style of a written introduction will carry over to the rest of the sermon whether it is written out or not. First impressions are crucial. If the audience perceives the sermon to be rambling, general, and repetitious at the start, its attention will quickly fade. If, however, the introduction is precise, organized, and interesting, it will put the audience in a "Let's hear more" frame of mind. Good introductions are written introductions because the discipline of writing is the best way to achieve, as Stewart says, "clarity of thought and perspicuity of style."

How about unconventional introductions? The overwhelming majority of sermon introductions will be rhetorical monologues delivered in the traditional way, but even the most conservative preachers get an occasional urge to try an "innovative" sermon introduction. Unconventional introductions generally fall into two categories: verbal and nonverbal. A widely quoted verbal introduction to the topic of world hunger goes something like this: "Twenty thousand people will starve to death today and most of you don't give a tinker's damn. Furthermore, you are more distressed at my use of the word 'damn' than you are about the twenty thousand who will die." It's a great opener, attention-getting, confrontational, relevant. An attention-getting nonverbal introduction to the same topic might involve flashing twenty graphic slides of starving people on a movie screen just before you step to the pulpit.

Needless to say, unconventional introductions must be carefully planned and meticulously executed. Rehearsal, especially of more theatrical nonverbal stunts, is mandatory. However, unless you have unlimited imaginative energy, preach only three or four times a year, or are married to a Broadway producer, don't plan on using innovative openers every week. If you do, chances are you'll wear out both your listeners and yourself.

Having dealt with these preliminary issues, we are ready to consider what actually goes into a successful introduction and how to put one together.

2

Make Contact

The car was dead in the driveway. No ignition. No lights. No horn. No nothing. I knew the battery wasn't that old, but what else could it be? I borrowed jumper cables from a friend, but no matter how I held, clamped, or jiggled them, nothing happened. Finally, defeated again by mechanical subtleties beyond comprehension, I called road service.

"Nothing to it," announced the mechanic sent by the local Sunoco station. "The battery is fine. What you need are new terminals. The old ones are corroded and won't conduct. They're not making contact." No wonder the cables wouldn't work.

Sermons are like my old Chevy: no contact, no start. I don't know how many contact points there are in an automobile ignition, but a sermon introduction needs four: the secular, the biblical, the personal, and the structural. Smooth-starting sermons depend on these four contacts. Before illustrating the four contact points in actual introductions, I will give a short explanation of each one.

Most sermons should begin with the life experience of the listener. I call this 'the secular' derived from the Latin word *saeculum*, which means "age" or "time." In its original context the word was used to refer to that which is temporal as opposed to eternal. It suggests the experience of life in the world, day-by-day, week-by-week. It is this temporal life that makes an effective contact point for the sermon introduction and provides the best way to grab attention and establish relevancy. Lloyd Perry states the issue well:

> [The] core thought of the introduction should be developed in terms of the daily living of the listeners. It should, therefore, meet the people where they are living. The sermon will later lead them to the cross for salvation, for sanctification, or service. The sermon thus begins with a secular discussion. . . .[1]

The second contact point of the introduction is the biblical. The introduction must move naturally from the life of the listener to the Word of God. It is at the point of biblical contact that many introductions go awry.

Many theologically conservative preachers wrongly assume that the biblical contact is all that is needed. They neglect the secular contact point and quickly lose the attention of the audience by plunging into what is perceived to be an academic, boring, and irrelevant Bible study. Theological liberals may be prone to the opposite error. Questioning either the Bible's authority or relevance or both, they may start with the secular and stay with it, never moving to the Word. In sermon delivery, the biblical contact must come *after* the secular, but it must inevitably come so that preaching not be reduced to religious punditry.

When it comes to the relationship of the secular and the biblical, it is very important to note that sermon delivery and sermon preparation take opposite courses. In preparation, the Bible comes first. Scholarly exegesis coupled with humble meditation lead to the application. While preparing the message, the preacher moves from the Bible to the newspaper. Sermon delivery is just the opposite. Successful introductions move from the newspaper to the Bible. Keep in mind that the same preacher must move both ways with every sermon.

The third contact point is the personal. Every person who listens to the sermon is asking the same question, "What does this have to do with me?" You may be as contemporary and relevant as *Newsweek* and as theologically solid as Isaiah himself, but if you fail to personalize the message, your preaching will have little ultimate effect. The personal contact point encompasses what the traditional speech communications textbooks call the "need" step in public speaking. Why do the individuals in the audience need this sermon now? How does it touch their hopes, aspirations, sins, or problems?

The fourth contact point is a bridge from the introduction to the body of the sermon. It guides the listener toward the structure of the sermon and, therefore, is called the structural contact point. Even though it may consist of only a sentence or two, it forms the crucial connection between the introduction and the unfolding of the message. It may or may not include a preview of the sermon's main points, but it will at least tell what the main points are: a set of principles, a series of examples, a list of warnings, a cluster of reasons, a series of steps in a process. The structural contact leads to the main body of the sermon by revealing to the audience what is coming.

We will discuss each of the four contact points in greater detail in subsequent chapters. The best way to grasp them now is to see them in actual introductions.

The following three paragraphs introduce "Confidence in Crisis," a sermon on Daniel 2, an Old Testament narrative passage. The first paragraph deals with the secular concept of "crisis." The second paragraph makes a biblical contact by describing the crisis faced by Daniel. The third paragraph personalizes with references to marriage, finances, health, and church. The very last sentence provides a structural contact with what is to follow. The main points will be "crises that illustrate important principles."

John Zakian, a former assistant to the Yonkers city manager, was quoted in the *New York Times* this week as saying, "Yonkers seems to survive on crisis. . . ." When I read that, it occurred to me that the whole world seems to survive on crisis. It seems like the media confront us with new crises every day. Central America, Lebanon, Poland are centers of crisis. Within our own borders we have crises in education, the economy, the environment. The dictionary defines a crisis as "a serious or decisive state of things . . . a decisive or crucial time, stage, or event." Even though American hostages were held in Iran for well over a year, the situation was always called the "Iranian crisis." William Safire pointed out that if a crisis is a problem requiring quick resolution, then a chronic crisis is a contradiction in terms. Whether or not a chronic crisis is possible, we live in a world of chronic problems that frequently take on crisis proportions.

Daniel lived in a world much like ours. There too, chronic problems constantly threatened to become dangerous crises, and Daniel 2 has all the elements of a major crisis. Nebuchadnezzar was the king—brutal, powerful, yet somewhat worried about the security of his rule, scheming to solidify his grasp on the throne. Near the king in the Babylonian government were the very influential and powerful astrologers and sorcerers whose origins went back to the beginning of time. For some reason Nebuchadnezzar did not trust his magicians and seemed to be looking for a way to break their power. A few of these wise men were young Jewish exiles walking the thin, dangerous line between service to government and loyalty to God. In this explosive situation, God saw an opportunity to reveal his world-embracing plan for history—not only to that generation but to all generations. So he gave Nebuchadnezzar a vision that set in motion a major crisis in Babylon in which Daniel would play the decisive role.

How do you respond in a crisis? Just as there are many types of national and international crises, there are various kinds of personal crises that can affect your life. In your marriage, you may have allowed unresolved difficulties to smolder in the background for too long and now they have flared up in a major problem.

Make Contact

The loss of a job or the failure of investments can throw
you into a financial crisis requiring radical readjustment
of your material expectations and lifestyle. Your health,
seemingly good, can change suddenly, bringing you
face-to-face with a serious operation or even death. The
church body itself goes through crises, times when
decisive actions are needed to deal with problems or to
claim opportunities. The crises of life are inevitable. The
question is not how to avoid them, but how to deal with
them. God wants you to have confidence in crisis.
Daniel 2 contains three separate but related crises that
illustrate important principles for benefiting from the
crises you face.

The next introduction is for a sermon on Matthew
18:21–35, the parable of the unmerciful servant. The secular
contact consists of a lengthy quotation concerning athletics.
The second paragraph relates the idea of the quotation to the
biblical text and includes some explanation of the text. The
personal contact in the third paragraph is rather brief. If
anything it could be more confrontational. Once again the
last sentence forms a structural contact and alerts the
audience to be listening for "qualities of a forgiving person."

In a *New Yorker* magazine article called "Attitude,"
Garrison Keillor tells about the fine points of slow pitch
softball, a game toward which he professes to take a
casual attitude. He says, "If a player's wife or girlfriend
wants to play, we give her a glove and send her out to
right field, no questions asked."
He then describes two memorable plays.

Bottom of the ninth, down 18–3, two outs, a man on
first and a woman on third, and our third baseman
strikes out. Strikes out! In slow-pitch, not even your
grandmother strikes out, but this guy does, and after his
third strike—a wild swing at a ball that bounces on the
plate—he topples over in the dirt and lies flat on his
back, laughing. Laughing!
Same game, earlier. They have the bases loaded. A
weak grounder is hit toward our second baseperson.
The runners are running. She picks up the ball, and
looks at them. She looks at first, at second, at home. We

yell, "Throw it! Throw it!" and she throws it, under-
hand, at the pitcher, who has turned and run to back up
the catcher. The ball rolls across the third base line and
under the bench. Three runs score. The batter, a fatso,
chugs into second. The other team hoots and hollers,
and what does she do? She shrugs and smiles ("Oh silly
me"); after all it's only a game. Like the aforementioned
strikeout artist, she treats her error as a joke. . . . They
have forgiven themselves instantly, which is unforgiv-
able. It is *we* who should forgive them, who can say,
"It's all right, it's only a game." They are supposed to
throw up their hands and kick the dirt and hang their
heads. . . .[2]

Preaching about forgiveness to our generation is a
tricky endeavor because when it comes to forgiveness
we are both experts and novices. Like the softball
players, we are experts at instantly forgiving ourselves,
but, like Jesus' disciples, we don't seem to know much
about forgiving others. In Matthew 18, Jesus tells his
disciples how to go about getting along with one
another. Beginning in verse 15, he gives them a step-by-
step plan for being reconciled when they are at odds.
But Peter's question in verse 21 reveals the great gulf
between what Jesus was trying to get across and where
the disciples were coming from. After hearing the
procedure of forgiveness, Peter asked another procedural question: how many times should we go through
the procedure with a difficult brother or sister? When
Peter asked the question, Jesus immediately saw the
problem. Peter perceived the issue as procedural, but
Jesus knew the issue was attitudinal. The parable of the
unmerciful servant deals with attitude. The punch line
is the last three words, "forgive your brother *from your
heart.*" Forgiveness is not essentially a matter of me-
chanics, a formula to be mindlessly applied, but an
issue of attitude. If your heart attitude is right, you
won't be counting the number of times you forgive.

The parable of the unmerciful servant is both negative and positive. It is negative in that it reveals the
marks of an unforgiving person, but from these characteristics we can derive the positive qualities of a
forgiving person. The power of this parable is in the

way it slices through our external preoccupation with doing the right thing to the heart issue of being the right kind of person. It can pierce your heart if you are willing to see yourself in it and to measure yourself by its standards. You must be honest enough to admit that you have some broken-down relationships in need of forgiveness. You must also be willing to forget, for the time being, all the actions you think you have taken to forgive or be reconciled, and focus instead on your own heart attitude. Are you really a forgiving person deep down inside? By God's grace you can be if you develop the qualities of a forgiving person that are illustrated in the parable.

Not all secular contact points consist of direct quotations. The following introduction begins with a humorous quip and some mild sarcasm. The transition to the biblical contact comes easily since the "obstinate children" idea is in the text itself (Isaiah 30). The personal contact is brief but pointed. The structural contact sentence alerts the audience to "three lessons" that can deliver them from obstinance.

It has been said that children are a real comfort in old age—and they make you reach it sooner too. It seems that some children have a greater ability to produce gray hairs in their elders than others. I'm sure you were not that kind of child and that you don't have any children like that, but I have heard that some exist. Such children used to be called "brats." But in our age of euphemisms, such terms are not permitted. Now, thanks to Dr. James Dobson, we call them "strong-willed children." Can you imagine an exasperated teacher shouting at a five-year-old monster, "You little strong-willed child!"

Throughout the Bible, God refers to his people as his family. Bill Gaither wrote a song that says, "I'm so glad I'm a part of the family of God." Christians are God's children, part of God's forever family. But the Bible also tells us that there are brats in the family of God. Isaiah calls them the "obstinate children." God's obstinate children are characterized by a desire to have their own way. They pray, "Not thy will be done but mine," and they are constantly testing the boundaries of obedience. God, like any loving parent, disciplines his strong-willed kids. Deuteronomy 8:5 says, "Know then in your heart that as a man disciplines his son, so the LORD your God disciplines you."

I believe all of us, at one time or another, fall into the category of God's strong-willed children. Were you intent on having your own way this past week? Do you ever test the boundaries of obedience? I also believe that if God had a reform school for us obstinate children, Isaiah 30 would be the curriculum. The curriculum contains three lessons, each one designed to transform the obstinate child into an obedient one. The message of Isaiah 30 is that even in your most obstinate moments, God can help you become obedient. Learning the three lessons of Isaiah 30 can deliver you from obstinacy to obedience.

The following three paragraphs introduce a message entitled "Bearing the Family Likeness." It is based on a passage from the Epistles, Ephesians 4:31–5:2. The secular starting point is simply a recitation of some well-known facts about the family. The biblical contact moves from sociology to the theology of Ephesians and then lists the Bible verses on which the sermon is built. The personal reference in the third paragraph contains a specifically evangelistic twist that will be pursued later in the sermon. In this case, the structural contact previews the two main points: belonging to the family and bearing its likeness.

The status of the American family has been a favorite topic of discussion for quite some time. According to some analysts, the family is in trouble. Others believe it is thriving. Everybody agrees it is changing. We know, for example, that families today are smaller than ever before. In my own family large families were the norm in previous generations. One of my great grandfathers had thirteen children. Today, however, our family of three children seems large. Families today are richer than ever. The headlines this week declared that family income is up over seven percent. Families are also more urban than rural. When America was founded, about ninety percent of families lived on farms. Today fewer than five percent are on the farm. When it comes to families, it seems, the only certainty is change.

Just as sociologists examine the changing fortunes of the human family, theologians study the dynamics of the spiritual family. Writing as a theologian in Ephesians, Paul describes how God's children can go about imitating their heavenly Father. In other words, he tells how Christians bear the likeness of the spiritual family to which they belong. Before he begins talking about human families in verse 22 of chapter 5, he alludes to the spiritual family at least five times in verses 1 through 20. He says Christians are dearly loved children (verse 1), who have an inheritance (verse 5), and may be called the "children of light" (verse 8). Furthermore, Christians have the privilege of calling God "the Father" (verse 20). So the Christian is concerned not only about the status of the human family but also about the spiritual family of God. Specifically, our twofold concern is how we become members of God's family and how we can come to bear the family likeness.

Family membership is a very personal concern. The status of the family has personal implications that touch us deeply. For example, it is little consolation to know that family income is up over seven percent if our own family income is down seven percent. The status of the family is a personal reality, not a statistical abstraction. It's the same with the spiritual family. Belonging to God's family and bearing its likeness are matters of utmost personal concern. The question boils down not so much to the status of the family but to your status in the family. What is your status in God's family? Are you really a member? If so, does your life obviously bear the traits of your family? The message of God's word from Ephesians today is that you can belong to God's spiritual family and bear its likeness.

No contact; no start. All four contact points are essential to every introduction. Omit the secular and you stand a good chance of losing the audience before you really get started. Omit the biblical and you have nothing to say. Omit the personal and the sermon drifts over the listeners' heads and out the back door. Omit the structural and your audience faces a rough ride to an unclear destination.

Now that we have seen the contact points in practice, we need to look at each one more closely.

3

Start with the Secular

Lewis B. Smedes has poignantly described the *dramatis personae* of the morning worship service:

> A man and woman, sitting board-straight, smiling on cue at every piece of funny piety, are hating each other for letting romance in their marriage collapse in a tiring treadmill of tasteless, but always tidy, tedium.
>
> A widow, whispering her Amens to every promise of divine providence, is frightened to death because the unkillable beast of inflation is devouring her savings.
>
> A father, the congregational model of parental firmness, is fuming in the suspicion of his own fatherly failure because he cannot stomach, much less understand, the furious antics of his slightly crazy son.
>
> An attractive young woman in the front pew is absolutely paralyzed, sure she has breast cancer.
>
> A middle-aged fellow who, with his new Mercedes, is an obvious Christian success story, is wondering when he will ever have the guts to tell his boss to take his lousy job and shove it.
>
> A submissive wife of one of the elders is terrified because she is being pushed to face up to her closet alcoholism.

Ordinary people, all of them, and there are a lot more where they come from. What they all have in common is a sense that everything is all wrong where it matters to them most. What they desperately need is a miracle of faith to know that life at the center is all right.[1]

Preaching must communicate the miracle of faith to the ordinary person. However, a sermon that rushes too soon to the miracle of faith runs the risk of losing the ordinary listener. You can avoid this common pitfall by starting with a secular, life-related contact point.

What could be more natural than encountering the listener first on his or her own level and then leading into God's Word? What could be more unnatural than launching into a religious oration hoping that somehow the listener will see the connection between religion and life? Yet it is precisely this unnatural, deadening technique that many preachers employ.

The following two paragraphs are typical of an introduction that begins with the biblical contact point without any contemporary reference. They were used to introduce a sermon on Zechariah 9:10 entitled "The King Who Commands Peace."

The words come from the prophet Zechariah. He was writing about the Messiah. In his view the day would come when the Messiah-King would come and institute peace throughout all of the world.

He would be a strange combination—this King. On the one hand He would be from sea to sea—to the ends of the earth (Zechariah 9:10). "How good and fair it shall be!" wrote Zechariah. How good indeed![2]

Compare the preceding quotation with the one that follows. This paragraph introduces a sermon called "Thank God for the Interruptions."

Working in his office in Minneapolis, Jess Lair, thirty-five years of age, collapsed with a heart attack. He had been driving for success —and succeeding—in a job he hated. In the hospital he had plenty of time to do some deep thinking. He reviewed his life and decided: "From now on I am never going to do anything that I do not deeply believe in." Mr. Lair and his family shifted to simple living. They now realized that they did not have to have all the things they once thought they did. Jess Lair enrolled in graduate school and earned a Ph.D. in psychology. Then the Lairs moved to Montana where he found a job teaching at a state university.

For his students he wrote the story of how his life was strangely turned around. He entitled his book *I Ain't Much, Baby—But I'm All I've Got*. It became a best-seller. It took a heart attack to get Jess Lair to seriously evaluate his life and get it turned around in the right direction.[3]

Now that you have read the opening words of the two sermons, which one would you like to hear? Which introduction was interesting? Which one was down-to-earth? Which are you most likely to quote in a sermon of your own? The choice is not difficult. The sermon that starts with the secular almost invariably starts better.

Where can you get ideas for good secular contact points? In his book *Biblical Sermon Guide,* Lloyd Perry lists no fewer than thirty-six types of "instruments or materials" for use in introductions, from a startling statement to a brief poem to a dramatic description.[4] His thirty-six types actually boil down to two categories: what you have experienced or read. Your experiences are richer and more varied than you think. They are your best source.

The secret is to see the connection between your reading and experiences and the sermon you want to preach. The creative preacher is the one who can see a link between next Sunday's sermon and the elements of his own life: this morning's paper, last week's visit to the dentist, or the felling of an apple tree in his back yard five years ago.

This ability to make connections is not an inherited characteristic or a spiritual gift as much as it is a mental attitude and discipline. Key elements in developing such a creative mind-set include maintaining a positive attitude, having a questioning mind, writing ideas down so you don't forget them, and lots of hard work. The connections between your experiences and reading and your sermon really are there waiting for you to see and articulate them.

Even the best secular reference, however, once identified, needs to be articulated. The idea must be distilled into words, the words into sentences, and the sentences into paragraphs. Every sermon starts with an opening sentence. Effective preachers concentrate on that sentence. The opening sentence characterizes the whole introduction and deserves the closest attention.

First, let the opening sentence *be* an opening sentence. Let silence separate it from all that precedes it, whether music, Scripture reading, or pulpit small talk ("Thank you Mrs. Murphy, for that truly wonderful solo."). It takes discipline not to muddle or mumble into the sermon. Good preachers are not afraid of silence, especially that moment of quiet immediately before the sermon's opening sentence that sets the sermon apart from the preceding item in the liturgy.

What follows is a list of one hundred opening sentences actually used in sermons.[5] Imagine yourself sitting in the pew ready to hear your pastor preach the sermon. Which of these sentences makes you want to hear more?

> One of the key words in the vocabulary of modern man is the word "freedom."

> On January 22, 1973, the Supreme Court was meeting in the nation's capital.

> These are days of crisis.

> Wasn't everybody expecting a resurrection?

> Christian culture is dead.

> Is the doctrine of the Trinity "pagan" and "a false, unbiblical doctrine"?

> The prophet Amos centuries ago warned against complacency, when he said, "Woe to you who are complacent in Zion" (Amos 6:1).

Start with the Secular

The question of divorce is a real and abiding problem in our society.

Isn't it funny the way life drifts along, and we drift with it?

If you wanted to destroy a society without the use of weaponry, how would you do it?

In order to have a happy and worthwhile life, it is necessary to have a faith to live by, a purpose to live for, and a self to live with.

A faithful member of one of our churches listened to a sermon preached on the text "Do not lay up for yourselves treasures on earth. . . ." He felt very inspired, and believing what he heard, made some decisions about his own life.

There is much confusion about the will of God.

Just exactly what is the Church about?

Paul Tournier capsulizes the human predicament in a phrase from his book, *Adventure in Living*. He says: "Man is capable of spoiling his life."

I am sure all of us believe in prayer.

A certain man spent most of his life on a South Pacific Island where the weather was always balmy and clear.

The mood of today is one of joy.

At first, this proposition may seem contradictory. (Referring to sermon title, "What the World Needs is Fewer Churches and More Bodies of Christ")

When I first realized that the Gospel reading for this Sunday was about marriage, I said, "Oh good, that should be easy to deal with."

"I give up. Lord, I'm sorry, but I can't take it anymore." (Monologue spoken by Moses to God during his unsuccessful negotiations with Pharaoh)

INTRODUCING THE SERMON

To those of you who have been taught in the Scriptures, the subject of this message sounds strange; for it seems to contradict all that we have been taught. (Referring to sermon title, "When God is Nowhere to be Found")

The poor church in Jerusalem was having a hard time of it.

One of my all-time favorite children's books is entitled *Alexander and the Terrible, Horrible, No Good, Very Bad Day*.

The chapter out of which this text is taken contains an account of Paul's conversion to Christianity, which he gave before Governor Festus and King Agrippa.

Notice the question. It is not, "How much do you give?" (Referring to sermon title, "How do you Give?")

Last July, when we held our Junior High Campout, one lad had a saying when things weren't as right as he supposed they should be, "It isn't fair." If he said it once he said it a dozen times.

Guideposts magazine tells the story of little Jamie Scott, who was trying out for a part in the school play.

"What the world needs now . . . is love, sweet love!" Many of you remember that song.

Why do smorgasbords have such great appeal to us?

Recent years have seen a deluge of what has been called self-help literature.

"Mr. Webster, will you tell me what was the most important thought you ever had?" The place was the Astor House in New York during the administration of President Millard Fillmore. Twenty young men, including Daniel Webster, then Secretary of State, were present for a dinner.

You may wonder how I can speak of "God's handicap" when the Scriptures assure us that God is able to meet our needs, that He sees and hears our plights and knows our situations, that He is a nurturer and a willing provider. (Referring to sermon title, "God's Handicap")

For the past several months, many Americans have been fascinated with the Rubik's cube.

Not all of us have wealth, but we all have burdens.

What do we do "when our loved ones let us down"?

According to *Time* magazine the three most commonly used drugs in the United States are (1) Tagamet for ulcers, (2) Inderol for high blood pressure, and (3) Valium for anxiety.

Even before His birth, Jesus' mission was made clear in the announcement to Joseph by the angel of the Lord.

If you're like me, you don't like change.

It was the summer of 701 B.C. Sennacherib had marched with his Assyrian forces, destroying the cities of Sidon and Phoenicia.

We see in our Scripture lesson (the Gethsemane experience) one of many times in the life of Christ when He experienced what all of us experience from time to time—and something that many people face all the time—that is, the experience of being alone.

With the rising cost of inflation, and an increasing number of people in America who are without work, no one seems to deny that America is in a recession.

My concern arises from the conclusion that we do not really communicate very well with each other most of the time.

A couple of years ago, I saw a television movie entitled, "It Happened One Christmas."

On the day before Thanksgiving several years ago we held a special worship service for shut-ins.

I have always wondered how wise those guys from the East really were.

INTRODUCING THE SERMON

The story of an English doctor is told by A. J. Cronin in the novel *The Citadel*.

In both the Old and New Testaments are many instances of undeniably miraculous healing.

As a child, when my conduct had not been exactly what it should have been, and I heard my mother or father say, "I have a mind to. . ." I would begin to shrink inside.

The twenty-seventh Psalm is a beautiful composition in which the poet expresses his ultimate trust and confidence in God.

A teen-aged girl was asked why she continued to practice so hard when her coach rarely put her in a game. She answered, "I want to be ready just in case I get to play." There come, I believe, in each of our lives, certain illuminating, decisive moments—moments when the direction our lives will take hangs in fateful balance.

Marriage has gotten a bad reputation through the last few years.

A woman was bitten by a dog suspected of having rabies.

Have you ever wondered why it is that some people seem to have to fall into hell, or to find themselves in hell, before they are willing to take God seriously and to believe that God wants to have a personal and meaningful and saving relationship with them?

John Steinbeck wrote a poignant story called "The Leader of the People."

Are you a recognizable Christian?

Back in the days of Julius Caesar, there was a Roman poet named Horace.

I have always been the kind of person who believes, as the Westminster Divines said in 1647, God "hath foreordained whatsoever comes to pass."

Start with the Secular

Have you been invited to a wedding lately?

If you have ever played chess, you know that the pawn is the least powerful and most expendable on the board.

During the past few weeks many of us have received in the mail a booklet from the Four County Nuclear Safety Committee called 'Indian Point, Emergency Planning, and You."

At a recent seminar on the psychological effects of the possibility of nuclear war, Dr. John Mack, a Pulitzer Prize-winning author who teaches psychology at Harvard, said studies show that many young people "have a sense of powerlessness about the transience of life . . . ."

In the February 1982 issue of *Psychology Today* magazine, Carin Rubenstein wrote a major article about the emotional health of nine geographic areas in America.

You've probably heard the old saying, "I love mankind. It's people I can't stand."

Mark Twain once observed, "A thing long expected takes the form of the unexpected when at last it comes."

One of the big differences between living in urban and rural America is the content of television commercials.

Today I have the dubious honor of preaching on what may very well be the most unpopular teaching of Jesus Christ in the church.

In 1963, the minister of the Christ Church in New York City published a book on the parables called *He Spoke to Them in Parables.*

In one of his Creative Leadership books, Lyle E. Schaller cites this statistic: " . . . approximately 93 million American adults identify themselves as Protestants, but the reported membership of all Protestant churches of all denominations in the United States totals less than 80 million—and this figure includes at least 10 million members who are under eighteen years of age . . . ."

According to the *Dictionary of American Slang*, a Johnny-come-lately is a "newcomer: anyone or anything that is tardy, specifically, a person who joins a group after the group's success seems assured and after his support is no longer needed."

Which are you, a starter or a finisher?

Problems between landlords and tenants are as old as history.

"If you're coasting, you're going downhill."

In Shakespeare's tragedy *Macbeth*, Act V, Scene 5, upon hearing the news of his wife's death, Macbeth responds with these lines. . . .

During the early 1960's Kwame Nkrumah was President of the West African country of Ghana.

Consistency is both a virtue and a vice.

How do you feel about yourself?

I love the comics, and one of my favorites is Andy Capp.

Guilt is the universal scourge of the human race.

What does the future hold?

I remember reading somewhere about a very unusual monastery in Portugal, perched high on a three-hundred-foot cliff.

The word "Christian" is found only three times in the New Testament.

Hup, two, three, four . . . . What are we all thankful for? Hup, two, three, four . . . . What are we all thankful for?

Two times in Scripture Jesus is wrapped.

Start with the Secular

When Andy Fielding graduated from high school last June, he took a poll among the senior class members.

The Italians have a very interesting New Year's custom.

We live in a world that puts a high emphasis on music.

Let me begin by retelling an ancient Greek myth.

As we come to the end of another year, we become invariably conscious of the passing of time.

Guilt is one of the mosf destructive feelings known to man.

In so many ways life asks us this important question: "What do you expect of yourself."

According to Henri Nouwen in the book *Reaching Out*, the most common complaint expressed to psychiatrists and clinical psychologists is loneliness.

How quickly and sharply Luke introduces Zacchaeus.

There are many different events we look forward to.

The historical setting for Labor Day is political.

Several years ago columnist Jack Anderson surveyed seventy thousand Americans to come up with a slogan that fit the generation of the 70's.

Original Bible writers and countless later commentators have elevated to special significance the hearing which a regional king, Herod Agrippa II, gave to the Apostle Paul.

King Saul had a problem, and the problem's name was Goliath.

As you walk in the door of a restaurant in Jackson, Mississippi, to the left there is a wall with hundreds of calling cards tacked on it.

Nothing has the power to stir the emotions of mankind like war.

A quick reading of the hundred opening sentences listed above reveals at least four common types of openers that are problematic.

First, there are the biblical references like "How quickly and sharply Luke introduces Zacchaeus."

What, you may be wondering, is wrong with starting with a comment about the text? Most such openers are dead on arrival (who cares about Luke's quick introduction of Zacchaeus?). For another, biblical introductions presuppose that today's audiences know something about the Bible and perceive it as relevant to everyday life, something no contemporary preacher can take for granted.

The truth of the matter is that despite all the Christian education of the last thirty-five years, churchgoers today are probably more biblically illiterate than ever before. If you have Luke and Zacchaeus in the opening sentence, half the congregation will probably think it is a reference to *Star Wars*. Passing references and allusions to sports events, television shows, and current events may be made in a sermon at will. But references to Bible characters and events require detailed and rudimentary explanation, or the audience is likely to miss them completely. Lament this fact if you must; ignore it at your peril as a communicator. Similarly, preaching today must prove the Bible's relevancy, not presume it. That is why secular references at the start of a sermon are much more likely to relate to the audience.

A second general type of opening sentence found in the list above is the religious. Religious openers do not refer directly to the Bible but nevertheless sound churchy. "On the day before Thanksgiving several years ago we held a special worship service for shut-ins." Preachers can be expected to talk about religious things because, after all, it's our business. But the ordinary people in the pews are not so interested in hearing about our world as in finding out what we know about theirs. Even so, religious openings can be successful if they are interesting or unusual like the following: "Today I have the dubious honor of preaching on what may very well be the most unpopular teaching of Jesus Christ in the Church." Or, "Christian culture is dead."

A third easily identifiable category of opening sentences is the historical. History can be made interesting, but you really have to work at it. As a general rule, the task of demonstrating relevancy increases the farther back in time you go. The following two openers are comparable: "Back in the days of Julius Caesar, there was a Roman poet named Horace," and "During the early 1960's Kwame Nkrumah was President of the West African country of Ghana." The second, however, is more recent and therefore probably more interesting. Begin your sermon with a history lesson only if all else fails. For maximum attention, lean toward current events and contemporary references as much as possible.

A fourth category of openers evident in our list includes references to the sermon title. An opening like that can work only if the listeners have read the title first and preachers should not assume that they have. If you choose to read the title, it becomes the opening sentence and may or may not be a good one. Appealing sermon titles are very rare. Most are either boring or cute. Consequently, most sermon introductions work well without mention of the title at all.

The miracle of faith can lift the ordinary person to extraordinary heights. Communicating that miracle is the task of preaching. A secular, life-related contact point at the beginning can give an ordinary sermon an extraordinary entry into the psyche of the listener and so begin the miracle of faith. Starting with the secular is so important to effective communication that our discussion of it needs to extend to the next chapter.

4

Spice Up the Secular

Once I saw a cartoon that showed a preacher standing in the pulpit as someone attached battery jumper cables to his ears. One parishioner remarked to another, "Sometimes the pastor needs a little help getting started."

Even the most apropos secular reference may need a little help getting the sermon off the ground. Merely starting with a secular point of contact does not guarantee you will have a relevant, attention-arousing introduction. The opening lines must generate interest or curiosity. It must avoid being bland, too general, or irrelevant to the topic at hand. The following opening sentences establish a point of contact with life issues but still fall flat:

> Why do smorgasbords have such great appeal to us? (Smorgasbords?!)

> Not all of us have wealth, but we all have burdens. (An anemic truism. Wealth and burdens are unrelated concepts unless you spell out the relationship.)

> A teen-aged girl was asked why she continued to practice so hard when her coach rarely put her in a game. She answered, "I want to be ready just in case I

get to play." There come, I believe, in each of our lives, certain illuminating, decisive moments—moments when the direction our lives will take hangs in fateful balance. (Nice try, but an uncompelling quotation followed by an unrelated platitude won't make it.)

We live in a world that puts a high priority on music. (How about a simple, "Everybody loves music.")

Suppose you have seen the connection between the secular point of contact and the thrust of the sermon. How can you be sure that when you use it to begin the sermon it will arouse attention and not produce boredom? Try concentrating on these two qualities: specificity (the use of detail) and relevance. They can make the introduction come alive.

Specificity is one of the most important and easily overlooked factors in effective communication. Consider the following opening sentence: "I remember reading somewhere about a very unusual monastery in Portugal, perched high on a three-hundred-foot cliff." It would be much more effective to specify the monastery's name and the name of the town. "St. Michael's monastery in San Cristo, Portugal, is perched high on a three-hundred-foot cliff." Specific references work better than generalities at drawing an audience in. They create sharper images in the minds of listeners, and they also enhance the speaker's credibility, making him sound like he knows what he's talking about.

The following two one-paragraph introductions demonstrate clearly the value of specificity. Both concentrate on the idea of "crisis."

These are days of crisis. Just listen to the newscast any day. You will hear of corruption in government, of murders, robberies, and all kinds of problems. Look at the reports regarding unemployment if you think it's over for poor people, if you think that the battle is fought, and the victory is won; look at the unemployment figures and you will see that we are caught up in serious crisis.[1]

John Zakian, a former assistant to the Yonkers city manager, was quoted in the *New York Times* this week as saying, "Yonkers seems to survive on crisis. . . ." When I read that, it occurred to me that the whole world seems to survive on crisis. It seems like the media confront us with new crises every day. Central America, Lebanon, Poland are the centers of crisis. Within our own borders we have crises in education, the economy, the environment. The dictionary defines a crisis as "a serious or decisive state of things. . .a decisive or crucial time, stage, or event." Even though American hostages were held in Iran for well over a year, the situation was always called the "Iranian crisis." William Safire pointed out that if a crisis is a problem requiring quick resolution, then a chronic crisis is a contradiction in terms. Whether or not a chronic crisis is possible, we live in a world of chronic problems that frequently take on crisis proportions.

The essential difference between these paragraphs is the number of details each contains. The first paragraph is general; the second, specific. The specificity of the second introduction consists of two names of people, five place names, one definition, one literary reference, and the citation of a paradox ("chronic crisis"). The more specific details you can work into the introduction, the better.

Specificity has one side effect: it will make the introduction longer. It takes more time to lay out details, but the time is worth it if you can gain the audience's interest. The best way to test for specificity is to write it out. On paper, it will be easier to spot vaguely worded paragraphs lacking detail.

Relevance is the other life-giving element of the introduction. An introduction must be relevant in two ways. It must be appropriate to the sermon and it must relate to the needs of the audience.

First, the secular reference that leads off the introduction must relate naturally to the sermon topic. Too often, in the weekly scramble to find a secular reference, preachers settle for one that has to be forced on the topic.

Here is an introduction that was used for a sermon on

2 Chronicles 32:31. The text deals with a test faced by King Hezekiah of Judah, and the sermon was entitled "Passing the Test."

> "Most of the pop psychology books make it seem as if there's an easy answer to finding happiness," says Dr. Jonathan Freedman, Columbia University psychologist and author of *Happy People*. "This is misleading and grossly oversimplifies the problem. Life is very complicated. You can't find happiness by following some simple recipe." Dr. Willard Gaylin, a New York psychiatrist, adds, "There are recipes for cookies, but not for people."
>
> Anyone who has lived, experiencing life's trials and problems, knows there are no simple answers. The difficulties encountered by Hezekiah show clearly the inadequacy of cookie-cutter solutions to life's tests and problems.

The quotation from Jonathan Freedman's book is a fine secular reference, but it's not all that relevant to the topic: "life's tests." The quotation is about happiness, not tests. The second quotation about life's complexities leads into the idea of testing, but the connection is forced.

Several years after this sermon was first preached, it was resurrected with the following, more relevant introduction.

> Anybody who has been through the American education mill knows something about tests and examinations. Pop quiz, final exam, comprehensives, and achievement tests—these terms still have the power to bring panic upon otherwise well-adjusted adults. I remember very few of the tests I took as a student, but there is one which stands out in my memory, one over which I am still gloating after eleven years.
>
> Greek was a prerequisite for entrance into seminary. In order to assure that all incoming students had had their Greek, the seminary devised a proficiency examination that was to be taken during the summer prior to admission. I was worried about that test. Most of the

people who took the test had two years of college Greek, but I only had one.

The test was to be divided into three parts: definitions of Greek words, recognition of grammatical forms, and translation of two or three paragraphs of Greek prose. The translation section was the most important part. Actually, the test was structured exactly like my college Greek final exam, which I had taken a few weeks earlier. In fact, to my surprise, the paragraphs for translation were identical! Needless to say, I passed the exam—just barely—and entered seminary with only half the normal Greek requirement.

Just as surely as testing is part of our educational system, it is also part of life. The Bible teaches that God will surely test you in the experiences and circumstances of life. God tested King Hezekiah, and he will test you.

Humorous introductions are especially prone to irrelevance. When used properly, humor can be a very effective lead-in, but the hardest thing about beginning with a joke is finding one that really fits the sermon topic. The following introduction uses a good joke but fails the relevance test.

In his book on angels, Billy Graham says he had never heard a sermon on the topic of angels. This may be due to the fact that many people view angels as an impractical topic. For most of us, practicality is of the essence. It reminds me of a story told by my wife's uncle. A man's home was surrounded by the rising flood waters of a nearby river. The waters rose past the windows of the house, so the man took refuge on the roof. A civil defense worker in a boat came by and asked if the man wanted to leave. "No," he said, "The Lord will provide." The waters got higher, and another boat came by. The rescuers insisted the man evacuate the area, but he refused. "The Lord will take care of me." Finally the waters rose all the way to the roof's peak. A rescue helicopter came and hovered over the house, but the man waved it away shouting, "The Lord will provide." Eventually the man was washed away and drowned. Upon arrival in Heaven, he said to St. Peter, "I thought you were going to take care of me." St. Peter replied, "You dummy, we sent two boats and a helicopter."

Like the man on the roof, many of us have trouble recognizing God's practical provisions for our lives. If what the Bible says about angels is true, nothing could be more practical than the study of angels. An angel might be at the controls of that helicopter!

The joke about the man on the roof is a good one. It can even be made to fit the topic. But that is precisely the problem. The fit is not natural. The joke is really about practicality, not angels. In the next example, the humorous anecdote fits in more naturally with the topic.

I remember reading somewhere about a very unusual monastery in Portugal, perched high on a three-hundred-foot cliff. You could only reach the monastery by a terrifying ride on a swaying basket that was pulled up by a single rope as several of the sturdy brothers strained and pulled together. One American tourist got nervous about half way up the cliff. He noticed that the rope seemed very old and frayed. He asked, "How often do you change the rope?" The monk who was in charge said, "Whenever it breaks!"

The American home seems to be in that kind of precarious situation! The basket is swaying, the rope is frayed and pulling apart. Down below we see a lot of wreckage from previous falls. According to a study completed at the University of Rhode Island, the home is a dangerous place to be—the most dangerous place to be outside of riots and wars. No less than thirty percent of all American couples experience some form of domestic violence in their lifetime. . . .[2]

For the naturally witty preacher humor can be an effective tool. The rest of us should use it sparingly and with care. As one wag put it, "One preacher uses humor and hits the target; another attempts it and shoots himself." Perhaps the serious business of preaching lends itself only marginally to joke-telling anyway. It may not be popular to say so, but our lust for funny preachers and sermons may betray an unbecoming shallowness in both pulpit and pew.

Not only must the introduction be relevant to the sermon topic, it must also relate to the audience. The introduction that sounded good Sunday morning, for example, may not be at all appropriate for the Wednesday afternoon service at the retirement home. Consider the following opener:

> In the February 1982 issue of *Psychology Today* magazine, Carin Rubenstein wrote a major article about the emotional health of nine geographic areas in America. To no one's surprise, the lowest psychological well-being in the country was found in the Middle Atlantic region: New York, New Jersey, and Pennsylvania. Rubenstein concluded: "People who live in Miserable Megalopolis rank last in their overall satisfaction with life and first in stress. They rank second worst in their outlook on life, second lowest in number of positive feelings and sense of personal competence, and fourth in negative feelings."

If this sermon ever goes on the road outside New York, New Jersey, and Pennsylvania, it will obviously need a new introduction.

The secret to relevant introductions is simple: know your audience. The parish minister is at an advantage here. In fact, any pastor who cannot figure out what relates to his own congregation had better change careers.

In summary, a successful introduction will start with the secular. Find secular references in your reading and experience that relate well to the sermon topic and to your audience as you know it. Give special attention to the opening sentence, and major on detail. Finally, hone your proficiency by the discipline of writing out the introduction.

Remember: no contact, no start.

In the last two chapters we have covered the first contact point, the secular, in some detail. We are now ready to consider the second: contact with the Bible.

5

Move to the Word

What makes a sermon relevant? Does a pithy, entertaining secular illustration guarantee a relevant message? In his book *The Integrity of Preaching*, John Knox points out that to be truly relevant, a sermon must be biblical.

> In a word, if we as preachers are not speaking to the needs of the contemporary world, it is a fair guess that we have not really heard the gospel of the early church. On the other hand, however much concern we may have about the contemporary world, that concern is not Christian except as it stems from the conviction that an event occurred in the first century in the light of which alone the meaning of the contemporary scene can be understood and in the power of which alone the community we seek can be realized. Only authentically biblical preaching can be really relevant; only vitally relevant preaching can be biblical.[1]

The second major contact point of the sermon introduction is the biblical. Without it, relevancy is impossible. God's Word— spelled with a capital W—must be the subject matter, the controlling source, of every sermon. The nonbiblical sermon does nothing more than add to the din of social commentary we are bombarded with from every conceivable source. The apostle Paul put it as succinctly as it can be put, "Preach the Word" (2 Timothy 4:2).

When it comes to making contact with the Bible, the key word is "context." A sermon has a biblical context. It is based on a biblical text, and the introduction must show how the sermon relates to that text. Here's an example of a sermon introduction that fails to establish an adequate link with its biblical context.

> I remember reading somewhere about a very unusual monastery in Portugal, perched high on a three-hundred-foot cliff. You could only reach the monastery by a terrifying ride on a swaying basket that was pulled up by a single rope as several of the sturdy brothers strained and pulled together. One American tourist got nervous about half way up the cliff. He noticed that the rope seemed very old and frayed. He asked, "How often do you change the rope?" The monk who was in charge said, "Whenever it breaks!"
>
> The American home seems to be in that kind of precarious situation! The basket is swaying, the rope is frayed and pulling apart. Down below we see a lot of wreckage from previous falls. According to a study completed at the University of Rhode Island, the home is a dangerous place to be—the most dangerous place to be outside of riots and wars. No less than thirty percent of all American couples experience some form of domestic violence in their lifetime. This helps explain why twenty percent of all police officers killed in the line of duty are killed while answering calls involving family fights. Six to fifteen million women are battered every year in our nation. No one knows how many children are battered and abused. We just know the figures are on the increase.
>
> The crippling psychological damage is beyond comprehension. The tragedy is that we tend to pass on to our children the very hurt and pain that we have received. The abused child grows to be a child abuser; the child whose self-esteem has been devastated tends to be the kind of parent who devastates and destroys

the self-esteem of his or her children. It is clear there is a bondage to the negative that enslaves and embitters millions of children, youth, and adults. Many homes resemble a battlefield.

Several years ago in *Family Week* magazine there was a cartoon, which was very interesting. It showed a husband and wife standing in opposite corners; each had an old-fashioned cannon aimed at the other. The fuse was burning away. There was a stack of cannon balls beside each cannon. The woman was standing there with her arms folded, the man was holding out the match and shaking it. It was evident there was going to be a terrific explosion in a matter of moments. Beneath the cartoon there were these words of explanation:

> A little boy went to his father with a question. He said, "Daddy, what causes wars?"
> The father put down his newspaper and thought a moment, then he said, "Suppose the United States and Great Britain should quarrel."
> "But we should never quarrel with Great Britain," said his mother.
> "I know that!" said the father. "I was just giving an example."
> "It was a misleading example."
> "It was not!"
> "Yes, it was!"
> The little boy turned away shaking his head and saying, "Never mind, now I know what causes wars."

The home is often a place of violence and like a battlefield. Perhaps right now, for you, the rope is frayed and wearing thin. It may be that, at this moment, you hear yourself asking, "What can I do to become a part of the healing, not the disease? What can I do to avoid hurting those for whom I care deeply? What can I do to become a more positive, constructive, caring, affirming person within the relationships which God has given me?"

In the book of Colossians, Paul gives us three great steps to follow that will lead to healthier and happier homes.[2]

The Colossians reference at the end of the introduction drops into the discussion out of thin air. What about Colossians? What makes it relevant to the topic? Why this passage of Scripture and not some other? Why Colossians and not the latest idea in *Psychology Today?* In short, what is the connection between Colossians and healthy homes? To be successful, an introduction must provide clear answers to such questions. It must establish a solid contact with the Word of God.

The following introduction (to a sermon on Hebrews 2:1–4) shows that only a few sentences are needed to anchor the message in the text. Note the italicized sentences.

> "Take any English word," writes Frederick Buechner, "even the most commonplace, and try repeating it twenty times in a row—umbrella, let us say, umbrella, umbrella, umbrella—and by the time we have finished, umbrella will not be a word anymore. It will be a noise only, an absurdity, stripped of all meaning. And when we take even the greatest and most meaningful of words that the Christian faith has and repeat them over and over again for some two thousand years, much the same thing happens. There was a time when such words as faith, sin, redemption, and atonement had great depth of meaning, great reality; but through the centuries of handling and mishandling they have tended to become such empty banalities that just the mention of them is apt to turn people's minds off like a switch. . . ."
>
> Sometimes the concepts of Christianity seem to be worn out and, as a result, we have a hard time paying attention to them. Familiarity may not breed contempt as much as it breeds inattention. *God wanted to communicate to the Hebrews the relevance and importance of the gospel, but it seemed like their minds were switched off. When it came to great truths of the faith they, just like us, seemed to be daydreaming, preoccupied, thinking about something else.* You know the feeling. Sometimes at dinner I find myself staring off into space, oblivious to my family, and then one of my kids will say, "Earth, calling Dad!

Earth, calling Dad!" and bring me back to reality. *The first four verses of Hebrews 2 are saying, "Heaven, calling the church! Wake up, down there!" The author digresses from his discussion of Christ and angels and says, "Pay attention! How shall we escape if we neglect so great a salvation?"*

We need to be reminded constantly and forcefully of the greatness of Christ and the gospel. This gospel, proclaimed by Jesus Christ, attested by God with miracles and the gifts of the Holy Spirit, received by the apostles, and experienced by the church is the most important issue in life. It is more important than buying a house, getting your degree, securing a job, or finding a spouse. Just like the Hebrews, we need to wake up and pay attention. All Christians—but especially those who think that they've heard it all before, that their experiences or affiliations or education or traditions have prepared them adequately—need to pay very careful attention. We evangelicals, who think we have paid better attention than others, need to pay particularly careful attention.

Are you paying careful attention to the truth of Jesus and his good news? Hebrews gives us three good reasons to pay better attention than we have.

The next introduction contains one complete paragraph (the second) that makes contact with the text, the parable of the two sons (Matthew 21:28–32).

The parable of the two sons got me thinking about starters and finishers. Which are you, a starter or a finisher? When you stop and think about it, you realize that all finishers had to have been starters, but not all starters are finishers. For example, everyone who finishes writing a letter to a friend started writing the letter at some point, but not everyone who starts to write actually finishes. How many half-written letters are on your desk? How many partially read books are on your shelf? During the last several months I've started to read about ten books, but have yet to finish one. Dieters and exercisers too know the difference between starting and finishing.

The parable of the two sons is about starting and finishing. The first son started poorly but finished well, while the second son started well but didn't finish at all. Jesus told this parable to the chief priests and elders of Israel, the religious establishment. When the Jewish clergy challenged Jesus' authority he, in turn, challenged their rejection of the obvious spiritual authority of John the Baptist. Then he told this parable, the first in a trilogy of parables dealing with his rejection by the very people who should have accepted him. The first son clearly represents the tax collectors and prostitutes, the spiritual outcasts, who change their initially negative response to God and end up doing his will. The second son is like the religious establishment, initially affirmative but ultimately disobedient. What Jesus is saying is that all of your verbal affirmations and good intentions, added together, can never equal discipleship. God is looking for starters who are also finishers.

How about you? When it comes to spiritual commitment, are you a finisher? Perhaps in the adult Bible class or church committee meeting you talk a good game, but you know, in the recesses of your own mind and conscience, that you're all talk. You know that you seldom if ever follow through on your commitments to God. You've had every opportunity and know all the right things to say, but when it comes to actual obedience, you always have an excuse that empties the meaning from your promises. The same idea applies to churches. Is this church a finisher or just a starter? We say we care and talk about outreach and stewardship, but how is our performance? God wants you to be a finisher as well as a starter. In the parable of the two sons Jesus shows what it takes to be a finisher.

The key to setting the biblical context is painstaking exegetical study. The preacher who can summarize the thrust of the text in a few words is the preacher who knows that text thoroughly—in English and the original language, in prayer and meditation. Bible knowledge, however, must be tempered by humility. Even though the sermon is based on the preacher's technical knowledge of the text, the purpose of the sermon is certainly not to display that knowledge. Recognition of this basic principle would save many congregations from the learned, vain, and boring Bible lectures that are passed off as sermons.

The preceding examples clearly show that setting the biblical context need not involve a long, detailed exegetical lecture. You must resist the urge to get involved in lots of interpretive, exegetical detail. The more detail you delve into, the deeper you will get, and the harder it will be to get out. The sermon should reflect the fruit of exegesis, not its process. Save the demonstration of your exegetical prowess for the classroom or Bible study group.

Remember, your audience is more biblically illiterate than you think, so deal with interpretive issues and details only when necessary for a basic understanding of the text. Even then keep it short and simple: a sentence or two devoted to identifying Bible characters you mention and defining theological terms that are unavoidable.

Of course, the more difficult or complicated the text, the more explanation it will need. The introduction that follows deals with a long, problematic Old Testament narrative. Remember the account in Genesis about Joseph and his estranged brothers? Joseph sabotages their saddle-bags while the brothers commute from Canaan to Egypt (Genesis 42–45). If you can avoid getting lost in explaining the action, you will discover a beautiful tale of forgiveness and reconciliation.

> In 1978, Mr. and Mrs. Robert Bristol of Dearborn, Michigan, took a vacation trip that made headlines around the country. Theirs was not an ordinary vacation. They traveled to California to visit an inmate at the California Men's Penal Colony. The inmate was the man who was convicted of raping and murdering the Bristol's twenty-one-year-old daughter Diane in 1970. When their daughter was killed the Bristols went through the normal reactions of grief and anger, but over the course of time they sensed a need to forgive. So they journeyed to the West Coast on a mission of

reconciliation. They met with their daughter's killer and talked for several hours. When it was over, they embraced him and commented to the press, "We personally have forgiven him completely."

This is an amazing story of reconciliation between people, but it is no more amazing than the account of Joseph's reconciliation with his brothers recorded in Genesis 42–45. Joseph—hated, sold into slavery, himself a prison inmate for several years—now at last met his brothers face to face. The way God brought about their reconciliation is one of the most instructive accounts in the Bible about the process of reconciliation between estranged people.

At first, the reconciliation of Joseph and his brothers appears to be a long, complicated, and confusing account of deception and delay. Joseph recognized his brothers the first time he saw them, but instead of immediately revealing himself, he kept one of them as hostage and sent the others home with the supplies they had come to buy. The brothers went home with the order from Joseph that they should not return to Egypt unless they brought Benjamin along. (Joseph was a full brother of Benjamin, but only a half brother to the rest.) Jacob was angry that Simeon had been left as the hostage, but the famine was so bad another trip to Egypt was necessary. Benjamin went along, but Joseph did not immediately reveal himself even when he saw his younger brother. Instead, he contrived a plan to force them to return to Egypt again. He made it look like Benjamin had stolen a silver cup and then stipulated that whoever had stolen the cup would become a slave. Joseph wanted to test his brothers to discover if they would abandon Benjamin to slavery as they has done to him. Finally, realizing his brothers had truly changed, Joseph revealed his true identity in the emotional scene in chapter 45.

Again we ask ourselves, "Why the delay? Why this complicated process of deception and false charges?" I believe there are logical reasons for Joseph's behavior. Joseph knew that his brothers would not be overjoyed to find him alive. Joseph alive was double trouble for the brothers: first they would be humiliated before their father to whom they had lied about Joseph's fate, and second, they would be in danger of Joseph's revenge. From his position of power, Joseph could easily have had his brothers done away with. So if Joseph had revealed himself immediately, they might have taken the supplies, returned to Canaan, never told Jacob that Joseph was alive, and never returned to Egypt. Furthermore, I believe Joseph really wanted to be reconciled to his brothers. He wanted God to help them work through the situation as God had helped him. Finally, Joseph wanted to see his brother Benjamin again. All of these factors must be kept in mind as we look at the details of the account.

You may not have as great crimes to forgive as the Bristol family or Joseph, but you too may have a need for reconciliation with someone in your life. You may have a broken relationship that needs mending today. God's will is for you to be right with others, and you can be. These chapters teach us the steps in the process of reconciliation.

Long or short, complicated or simple, familiar or obscure, your text must be introduced as well as your topic. The development of the text's main ideas occurs in the body of the sermon. But you need to establish an initial contact with the text in the introduction. It shows how and why the sermon really is biblical.

6

Link with the
Sermon Series

I have no figures to prove it, but I'm fairly certain that most preachers preach series of sermons. The series, whether a six-week Lenten study of the life of Jesus or a three-year exposition of Romans, lends an invaluable sense of direction to the pulpit ministry. Furthermore, it answers the question of questions: What am I going to preach on next week?

A second major issue in setting a sermon's context involves putting it in its place in a series. Actually, contextualizing the sermon in its series is another part of making contact with the Bible. Contact should be established with both the passage at hand and the longer text of the series.

The late Martyn Lloyd-Jones, series preacher *par excellence*, had this to say about sustaining a series.

> . . . [while the] tendency to be too long in giving a synopsis of the previous sermon must be firmly resisted, a summary is nevertheless essential for the people. It will help all of them, even those who attend regularly; and for strangers who attend, it is essential. So you must show the context of this particular sermon in the series, and its relationship to the whole, and perhaps throw out a hint of what is going to follow. But

it [this sermon] must be an entity in itself—this is most important.[1]

The first sermon in a series should have a dual-purpose introduction. The series, as well as the sermon, needs to be introduced. For example, in a series on Galatians with one message for each chapter of the book, the following paragraphs introduced both the series and the first sermon on chapter 1. The opening quotation and first three paragraphs deal with the whole series, while the last two paragraphs focus on the theme of the first chapter.

In *The Other Side* magazine, John Alexander gives the following account of a visit to Haiti:

> Recently I was in Haiti and took a walk through a market in a very poor section. It was in a shantytown, and shantytowns don't have sewers. The stench was unbearable. And food was being sold. The crowd was so dense I could hardly move. Some of the kids had red hair, and black kids usually don't have red hair unless they're starving. The night before, I'd taken a walk not far away, but the number of prostitutes had driven me away: whenever you have rich men in sight of extreme poverty, you have prostitutes.
>
> Now I'd seen all that before. A lot of times. But this time I couldn't stand it. I went home and took a nap. Sometimes I'd like to take a nap for the rest of my life. Not that I'm suicidal. But I'd sure like to shut the truth out, somehow. It's too costly.
>
> And that, of course, is the problem. The problem isn't evil people (though there's no shortage of them). The problem is that almost everyone is taking a nap.

John Alexander is right in pointing out that on many issues far too many Christians are dozing in the slumber of escapism. This observation is valid not only in terms of social ethics but also in theology. In Galatians 3:1, Paul refers to the Galatians as "bewitched." It's as if they had been hypnotized into semi-consciousness toward the truth of the gospel. They were in the process of trading the gospel of grace, the bedrock idea of Christianity, for a christianized version of Jewish legalism. They needed to wake up to what was happening.

Galatians is like a blasting alarm clock in the grey light of early morning. The alarm's racket racks our nerves until we shut it off, but afterwards we are grateful for the service it has performed, perhaps because we have an early appointment to keep. So it is with Galatians. Its message is harsh and shrill, but after understanding it, we are appreciative like the man in the aftershave commercial who says, "Thanks! I needed that!"

In the strongest possible terms, Paul wants to remind the Galatians of the essential truths of the gospel that they were in danger of abandoning. These are the same churches Paul personally founded, along with Barnabas, on his first missionary journey. Now, a year or two later, the infant churches at Iconium, Lystra, and Derbe were being influenced by Judaizers, teachers who wanted to make salvation conditional upon keeping the Jewish laws. They said God would save you only if you kept the religious laws of the Old Testament. The Judaizers told the Galatians that they, not Paul, represented the position of the Apostles of the mother church in Jerusalem. The Judaizers are the prototype for all the legalists in the history of Christianity who have tried to make salvation and Christian growth dependent on our works. As Paul points out in verse 7, the churches were in confusion over the questions of religious authority (Whom should we believe?), the nature of the gospel (How are we saved?), and the Christian life (How shall we act?). In this letter Paul deals with these issues. He touches on religious authority in the first two chapters, on the doctrine of the gospel of grace in chapters 3 and 4, and, finally, on practical Christian living in chapters 5 and 6.

The first part of Galatians deals with the question of authority because the Galatian Christians did not know whom to believe. Paul said one thing and the Judaizers another. The same problem exists today, only now it is much worse. Literally hundreds of "Christian" philosophies, denominations, and cults claim to have authority. The Galatians were lucky to have only two options to choose from! Not only are there many conflicting claims to authority in our society; there is also a strong dislike for authority. Many people want to replace authority with autonomy. Harry Blamires has written, "We move in a world in which thinking and feeling alike are coloured with a strong distaste for authority unparalleled in history." Against this backdrop, the apostle Paul insists that the gospel of Jesus Christ has an implicit authority to which we must submit. "If we cannot accept the gospel because of its superior truth," writes Clark Pinnock, "we must accept it because of its superior authority."

Perhaps you are confused like the Galatians, not knowing whom or what to believe. Perhaps you've been turned off by authority claims that you once accepted, or you may be facing the futility of trying to be your own authority. Paul's message is clear: you can confidently put your faith in the superior authority of the gospel. This superior authority is evidenced by the gospel's power, its permanence, and its origin in revelation.

The introduction to the second sermon in the same series follows. Notice that even though much less attention is given to the book as a whole, an effort is made to maintain continuity.

Harold Myra, the publisher of *Leadership* magazine tells this story:

> I was eating dinner with a friend one year ago when he told me what had just happened to his church on the West Coast. People had been upset with the pastor and wanted to get rid of him. They called a special meeting, and one by one, they publicly stood up and told all the reasons they didn't like him and his performance. Sitting in the congregation listening to all this was the pastor's eleven-year-old son and, of course, his wife.
>
> The image of this story stayed in my mind for months. How could something so cruel and thoughtless happen in a church? . . . other men in other professions may get fired, but seldom with such exquisite humiliation, and certainly not in front of their families.
>
> This is just one of the many horror stories I've heard the last two years while working on *Leadership*. Reading

the articles pastors and others in ministry have sent us
has confronted me again and again with the frequency
of their traumatic experiences.

In one sense, Galatians is a study case in pastoral
trauma. In the book we find Paul struggling with
unexpected problems in his young missionary career.
He undoubtedly had thought that the churches of Asia
Minor were firmly established and on the right track
toward growth and maturity. But just months after
returning to Antioch he began to receive disturbing
reports from Galatia. Where he had once been held in
high regard, he was now under attack. His preaching,
once accepted, was being questioned. The churches he
and Barnabas had founded in the face of opposition and
illness were in danger of going down the proverbial
drain. The emphatic, urgent tone of Galatians shows
the depths of Paul's concern and his pain.

In chapter 2, the apostle continues his discussion of
religious authority, sharing more details of his relationships with the Jerusalem church and the other apostles.
He claims that all his relationships and actions were
based on one unchanging principle. He states that
principle in verse 16, the key verse to the whole book:
"A man is not justified by observing the law, but by
faith in Jesus Christ." Since the theological implications
of this principle are brought out in chapters 3 and 4, I
want to consider chapter 2 in the more personal terms of
Paul's pastoral trauma over the situation in Galatia.

In the very churches he founded, Paul was personally
attacked and his teaching called into question. Yes,
even missionaries and pastors have their ups and
downs and struggles. In my own ministry I've gone
through some fire. I've encountered an intransigent
ordination council that didn't care for my theological
views. It was disheartening, to say the least, to be
temporarily denied ordination. Needless to say, clergy
catastrophes don't have an altogether wholesome effect
on churches either. I have seen the unhappy aftermath
in a church whose pastor was "asked to leave." When
pastors get together at meetings there are hushed
conversations during coffee breaks about church splits

and fights and firings. I assure you, it's the most dismal gossip on earth. Even though no one wants it to happen, it happens. In a recent poll, sixty percent of the ministers said they had experienced a traumatic event in their professional lives that they found extremely difficult to accept. No pastor wants it to happen, and no church wants it, but it happens anyway. It even happened to Paul and the churches of South Galatia. It can happen to you and me unless we pay attention to the principles of Galatians 2. Here we learn some ways to avoid the tragedy of pastoral trauma.

After two or three messages in a series, the audience starts to become somewhat familiar with the biblical material. Even so, each message should have a few remarks relating to the larger context of the series. The fifth sermon introduction in the Galatian series follows. Notice especially the italicized sentences, which relate to the larger series context.

In 1936, an NBC radio engineer, Claude Fetridge, came up with the idea of broadcasting, live of course, the departure of the swallows from the famous roost at Mission San Juan Capistrano. As everyone knows, the swallows always depart on St. John's Day, October 23. NBC made all the elaborate preparations for the event and sent a broadcast crew to the mission, but the swallows left a day ahead of schedule, on October 22. As a result of his experience, Fetridge coined what is known as Fetridge's Law, which states, "Important things that are supposed to happen do not happen, especially when people are looking." You have probably experienced Fetridge's Law firsthand when you started your car in the repair shop and it did not make the funny noise it had been making for the last six months.

Sometimes Fetridge's Law comes to mind when I consider the growth of the church and the progress of our Christian lives. Important things that are supposed to be happening do not seem to be happening. *Paul undoubtedly felt this way when he looked at the Galatian churches. In chapters 5 and 6, he turns his attention from doctrine to practical living.* He states the most important practical reality of all in verse 6 of chapter 5: "The only thing that counts is faith expressing itself through love." *Instead of concentrating on what really counted, the Galatians had entangled themselves in legalistic controversies.* How easy it is to get sidetracked onto less important issues. Some Christians are still preoccupied with legalism, others with activism or Christian busyness, others by spiritual gifts or personality comparisons or money or dieting or a host of other lesser concerns. We all need to be reminded that "the only thing that counts is faith expressing itself through love."

When you look at your own life, do you find what really counts, faith expressing itself through love? Or do you discover, like the Galatians, that your life has become a routine rooted in the less important and your Christian service a joyless religious charade?

In Galatians 5, Paul employs three powerful action verbs to describe what is involved in a life that, according to verse 25, keeps "in step with the Spirit." With the Spirit's power, you can make the important happen if you stand firm (verse 1), run well (verse 7), and serve in love (verse 13).

You can maintain the continuity of even a long series of sermons if you take care in each introduction to relate the current sermon and Scripture to the larger context of the series and its text. Keep in mind the following points.

1. The first introduction in the series is the most important. It may be twice as long as an ordinary introduction.

2. The amount of attention given to the context of the series decreases as the series progresses.

3. The attention devoted to series context will vary depending on the type of biblical material. Closely reasoned arguments like those in Romans and the Prophets will require more week-by-week development than the more

disjointed pericopes of the Gospels and the Old Testament narratives.

4. As Lloyd-Jones pointed out, each sermon must be a unique entity, more a self-contained sitcom than a running soap opera.

The consistent, disciplined preaching of the Bible in sermon series is not only possible, but greatly needed in the church today. The greatest need of all, however, is for distinctly biblical preaching. At the start of every sermon, in its introduction, the audience must be made aware that what is about to be said is no word of man, but the Word of God. The contact between Bible and sermon, forged in the study, must be clearly displayed and unapologetically proclaimed in the pulpit.

7

Touch Home

Who is the sermon for? This is a fundamental question, and a preacher's answer—whether consciously thought out or unconsciously assumed—will color the whole fabric of the pulpit ministry.

Is the sermon an outlet for the pastor, a chance to demonstrate biblical knowledge or ventilate pastoral frustrations? If so, we would expect more preachers to prepare sermons even on the weeks they were not scheduled to preach.

Is the sermon, perhaps, for God's benefit? Can the whole preaching enterprise be spiritualized into a liturgical offering to God? Certainly God can get along perfectly well without our sermons.

No. The sermon is for the congregation. It exists to bring conviction or information or hope to the ordinary people who hear it. If it fails to touch them, it has failed utterly.

So far we have considered two of the sermon introduction's contact points. The secular contact establishes the sermon's relevancy to temporal matters while the biblical contact establishes its authority.

The third contact is the personal. It touches home with the listener. Every sermon needs to do this. If a sermon fails to engage the listeners in their need and to relate to their sins and failures, their fears and hopes, it is both a homiletical and a pastoral failure. Phillips Brooks once said that the ability to discern the heart and mind of a congregation is a "wise and sympathetic instinct. To cultivate that instinct, to learn to feel a congregation, to let it claim its own from him, is one of the first duties of a minister. Until you do that you may be a great expounder, a brilliant 'sermonizer,' but you cannot be a preacher."[1]

Early in the sermon the listener must be convinced not only that the sermon is relevant "to our generation" and that it is biblical, but also that it bears directly on his or her own life now. The sermon must make personal contact. It is not as difficult as one might imagine. The sermon introduction that truly touches home will usually be marked by four specific characteristics.

1. It will address universally felt needs of people.

2. It will engage the particular audience at hand.

3. It will recognize and include the various groups in the audience.

4. It will get downright personal through use of the second person pronoun.

First, effective introductions address the universally felt needs of people. People are different; but they have many things in common. Some temptations, according to the apostle Paul, are "common to man" (1 Corinthians 10:13). The sermon introduction begins to touch home as it includes within its scope the issues faced by most, if not all, the members of the audience. Every member of the congregation is a member of a family; everyone can relate to the issues of physical health; virtually everyone uses money; everyone has a relationship with God whether he or she knows it or not. Effective, personal preaching involves addressing these basic, universal issues week after week.

Notice how the following introduction touches home in the fourth paragraph by addressing the basic needs of "something to believe in" and "someone to turn to." The sermon text is Hebrews 4:14–5:10.

> Access to the seat of power has been a political quest throughout history. Meetings with presidents, papal audiences, appointments with prime ministers are diligently sought and greatly coveted experiences. In his novel *1876*, Gore Vidal describes the imperial palace of nineteenth-century France, "where grown men and women used to spend their days and nights plotting to arrange, as if by accident, five minutes alone with the Emperor on the stairs, in a garden, anywhere that the imperial quarry might for an instant be snared and used in order to rise in the world."
>
> The quest for access to the seat of power continues today. One of the most powerful people in Washington must be the one who sets up the appointments with the President—the person who decides who will meet with the President and for how long. Unfortunately, even the people with the best ideas may never get a chance to express them to anyone who matters. I'm sure that somewhere in the back of your mind you may have some request or idea that you would share if you ever had the chance to speak with someone who is very influential or powerful. The trouble is that few of us feel very confident about our ideas and even fewer get the chance to express them to powerful people.
>
> One of the most revolutionary ideas of Christianity is that not only can ordinary people like you and me gain confidence in our beliefs, but we can take all our ideas, beliefs, and dreams directly to the top—not to the top of the political or military or business worlds, but to the top of the universe itself. According to the Bible, confident belief and access to the top are made possible by Jesus Christ. Hebrews describes Jesus as our great priest. In other words, as it says in verse one, he is

appointed to represent us in matters related to God. Two contrasting dimensions of his priesthood are emphasized. Not only is he transcendent, exalted, and high, he is also human, sympathetic, and accessible. Because he is transcendent, he is someone to believe in; because he is human, he is someone to turn to.

In those moments when you are most honest and candid with yourself, I'm sure you realize that there are two things in this world you need more than anything else: something to believe in and someone to turn to. At different times in our lives we are guided by certain ideas and presuppositions. Unfortunately, we often find those ideas to be unreliable. They become outdated, inadequate to explain our lives, or worse yet, just plain unworkable. The same is true of people. We put our confidence in people. Even though it's stupid, we do it anyway. And then, inevitably, we are disappointed in their performance. Perhaps today you are facing the bankruptcy of ideas you once thought valid or the unreliability of people you once trusted. Perhaps at one time you believed that being married was the key to happiness or that a certain job would be a sure road to success. Now, however, you're disillusioned. Perhaps you trusted a friend's discretion or pinned your hopes on one of your children and now you are completely disappointed.

No matter where you find yourself today, the message of the Book of Hebrews is vitally relevant: Jesus Christ offers you something to believe in and someone to turn to.

By specifying the areas of personal relationships, marriage, job, and children, the preceding introduction uses a shotgun approach to hit everyone in the audience. No one is excluded, except possibly grade school children. (You can't do everything.)

Personalizing the sermon in the introduction involves not only bringing up the universally felt needs of individuals, but also engaging the needs of the audience as a group. While the individuals in the audience have personal needs, the group itself has a distinct personality as well. The congregation is a particular group in a particular place at a specific point in time. Speak to that real group in front of you, not to some imaginary group. Too many preachers stand up in church and preach to the world.

The following two paragraphs open an Advent sermon on Luke 2. Notice how the second paragraph takes on the audience by referring to "we Evangelicals."

> Christmas means different things to different people. For students and teachers Christmas is a welcome break from the academic grind. For merchants it's the season that makes or breaks the fiscal year. For children it's the joy of anticipation. For the gourmet Christmas means holiday feasts and fine wine. For travelers Christmas is a season in the sun and sand of tropical climes. For football teams it's bowl time. For basketballers it's the holiday tournament. For an increasing number of Christians, Christmas has become the day before the post-Christmas conference. For you, I'm sure, Christmas must mean one or some or all or none of the above. As I survey the frantic Christmas scene I can't help but wonder to myself, "Does anyone really know what this holiday is all about?"
>
> Of course, we Evangelicals think we know all about Christmas. We know that the Virgin Birth is one of the fundamentals of the faith. We know all about Joseph's divorce and annulment options in dealing with his pregnant fiancée. We certainly know that the wise men didn't come to the stable on Christmas but arrived sometime much later and that there may have been two or five or fifteen of them rather than just three. We know all about Christmas—or do we? In spite of our fundamental theology and annotated Bibles, occasionally even in church I am still bothered by the question, "Does anyone really know what this holiday is all about?"

Preach to *your* congregation, not someone else's. What could be more ludicrous than for a white, suburban, middle-class Southern Baptist to denounce the sins of urban welfare cheats or for a liberal New York Episcopalian to rail from the pulpit about the backward racial attitudes of white southerners? Yet this happens all the time, and it is what most congregations expect to hear. Real prophets attack the bigotry, parochialism, and expectations of their audiences. False prophets never engage their audiences, probably because they themselves have not really struggled with the Word of God.

A third characteristic of the introduction that touches home is that it recognizes the various groups within the congregation. Every congregation is composed of many subgroups. How many students, working mothers, retirees, commuters, farmers, or military personnel are in the audience? Every group does not need mention in every sermon, but by mentioning a group or two each week, the preacher serves notice that he is aware of the groups and is sensitive to their unique needs.

A fourth characteristic of effectively personalized sermon introductions is the use of the second person pronoun. The following paragraphs formed the introduction to a sermon on the parable of the ten virgins (Matthew 25:1–13) entitled 'Keeping Watch." Notice how the third paragraph uses the word *we*.

> Mark Twain once observed, "A thing long expected takes the form of the unexpected when at last it comes." I believe this statement to be substantially true. For example, over the years that nations have put crude oil to industrial use, people knew that the supply of oil was unrenewable, a resource that would someday run out. But the actual experience of oil's limits in the early 1970's seemed completely unexpected. "A thing long expected takes the form of the unexpected when at last it comes." Consider another example, that of nuclear war. For almost thirty years we have expected it, but I am sure that if and when it occurs, it will be the most unexpected event in history.
>
> The dictum, "A thing long expected takes the form of the unexpected when at last it comes," has another

powerful, personal application. There is one thing that you expect for your entire life, but when it comes it will inevitably be unexpected: your own death. Paradoxically, death is the most expected and unexpected event of all. In the realm of faith, no theological reality fits Mark Twain's observation more perfectly than the second coming of Jesus Christ. The long-expected Second Advent will certainly take the form of the unexpected when at last it comes. Jesus knew this to be the case, so throughout his teachings, in both discourses and parables, he exhorted his followers to be ready, on the alert, watchful for his return. This is the point of the parable of the ten virgins, simply and practically stated in verse 13, "Therefore keep watch, because you do not know the day or the hour." The parable comes right in the middle of what is known as the Olivet Discourse, the most detailed teaching the Lord gave about end-time events. He hints that his Second Coming will be delayed and encourages his disciples to be constantly and consistently ready for his appearance.

For us, Christ's coming is a long-expected event. But we must be careful that this long-expected event not become an unexpected event. In short, we must be ready. And it seems to me that this readiness should make a tangible difference in our lives. We might say we are ready for Christ's return, but could a neutral observer see any difference between how we live and the lives of those who don't believe in Christ? Are we really ready for Christ's appearing? Not only do we need to be watchful for his Second Advent, we should also be ready for him when he comes to challenge, convict, judge, or encourage our lives. We must be ready also to face him when we die. For some people the coming of Christ, in whatever form it takes, is a long-expected joy, but for others it is an unexpected catastrophe. Since we do not know when Christ will come, we must keep watch. Our lives must be characterized by the actions of watchfulness illustrated by the parable of the ten virgins.

Rewritten using the second person pronoun, the third

paragraph takes on a more urgent and personally challenging tone.

> For you and me, Christ's coming is a long-expected event. But we must be careful that this long-expected event not become an unexpected event. In short, you must be ready. And it seems to me that this readiness should make a tangible difference in your life. You might say you are ready for Christ's return, but could a neutral observer see any difference between how you live and the lives of those who don't believe in Christ? Are you really ready for Christ's appearing? Not only do you need to be watchful for his Second Advent, you should also be ready for him when he comes to challenge, convict, judge, or encourage your life. You must be ready also to face him when you die. For some people the coming of Christ, in whatever form it takes, is a long-expected joy, but for others it is an unexpected catastrophe. Since you do not know when Christ will come, keep watch. Your life must be characterized by the actions of watchfulness illustrated by the parable of the ten virgins.

It is surely a mystery why many preachers opt for the anemic *we* when *you* would provide considerably more power and poignancy. Imagine the prophet Nathan confronting David with the Bathsheba affair and saying, "We are the men!" Nathan pointed his finger and said, "You are the man!" (2 Samuel 12:7). Preachers today need to speak with the same courageous audacity.

It might be argued that the use of *you* creates too much distance between the pulpit and the pew, destroying "common ground" with the audience. But common ground can be established more effectively in other ways. Saying, "I am tempted as you are," is certainly stronger than saying, "We are all tempted."

The use of *you* offers another advantage to speakers of English that should not be overlooked. Since *you* can be either singular or plural, it can refer to the whole audience and its individual members at the same time. The listeners make the application for themselves. If the preacher says, "You must be ready to face God when you die," some listeners will think of the readiness of the group (*you* plural). Others, for various reasons, not the least of which might be the prompting of the Holy Spirit, might take *you* very personally (*you* singular). No such advantage exists for *we*. It is always more general than particular, always plural, forever vague.

Every person who listens to the sermon wants to know what it means for his or her life. The sermon introduction that is both relevant and biblical must also make contact with the personal needs of the people, considered both as a group and as a unique gathering of individuals. No contact, no start. That applies to personal contact with the lives of the listeners too.

8

Build a Bridge

New York has been called a city of bridges, and anyone driving in the area knows the importance of all those bridges. Those of us on the east side of the Hudson must plan our westward excursions carefully, taking into account which bridge is closest with the lowest toll and the least potential for traffic jam. I can see Rockland County across the river from my office window, but getting there could be a time- consuming, unnerving hassle.

Getting from the introduction to the main body of a sermon can also be a hassle. If it is to succeed, even the most relevant, biblical, personal introduction must lead naturally to the main ideas of the sermon. The introduction's fourth contact point, the structural contact, exists to bridge the gap between the introduction and the points of the sermon. From the vantage point of the introduction, the preacher may clearly see the distant shore of the sermon itself, but the bridge must still be built and the audience transported across it. The audience must see a logical connection between introduction and sermon body. This contact point is "structural" because it refers to the structure of the sermon as a public address.

While the structural contact point is fourth and last in the delivery of the introduction, it must be considered very early in its preparation. Most journeys begin with the destination in mind. Sermon preparations begin with Bible study that yields particular ideas that become the points of the sermon. Identifying these points is the crucial element in making the structural contact.

The sermon's main idea, or proposition, as it is often called, ties these exegetical points together. The secular idea that begins the introduction is related in some way to the proposition, and so are the other contact points we have discussed so far. Of course, anybody who has ever prepared a sermon knows that these steps seldom occur chronologically. The order is logical. In the course of preparation, the ideas often come all at once.[1]

When the preacher tells his audience what the points of the sermon are, he lets them know what is coming. He shows them both the bridge and the ultimate destination so they can keep from getting lost. If he fails to show them where they are going, he should not be surprised if some of them fail to arrive at the destination. The points of a sermon usually are points of application and can be categorized as *lessons, warnings, examples, principles,* etc. Lloyd Perry calls these "key words" and lists no fewer than sixty-eight examples.[2]

The structural contacts that follow are from the introductions to six sermons on Isaiah 28–33. Notice that the plural nouns (key words) identifying the main points are italicized.

> Death is inevitable and judgment follows it. Isaiah 28 teaches you how to take positive *steps* now in order to avoid the negative consequences of God's judgment later.

> There are dangers on being part of the I'm-OK-you're-OK evangelical world. Isaiah's list of *dangers* serves as a warning to us residents of Zion.

Even in your most obstinate moments, God can help you become obedient. Learning the three *lessons* of Isaiah 30 can deliver you from obstinacy to obedience.

You must abandon the fantasy world in which you are living. Isaiah 31 gives clear *directions* on how to get out of fantasyland.

God offers you the extraordinary possibility of becoming a kingdom person. You can develop a kingdom character by living the kingdom character *traits* described in Isaiah 32.

God wants to deliver you. Isaiah 33 tells the essential *truths* about the deliverance God has for you.

Considering the structural contact point of the introduction invariably brings up the wider issue of the relationship between the exegetical process and the composition of the introduction. Exegesis comes first and results in the sermon's main points. This exegetical process is limited by the scope of the text itself. Different preachers may come up with different arrangements of the material or different emphases, but such differences are limited by the text if the sermon is to be truly expositional.

But while the exegetical possibilities for a given passage are limited, the number of possible introductions is almost unlimited. Furthermore, in the process of sermon preparation, a dynamic interaction occurs between the exegetical process (and the points it yields) and the introductory idea chosen by the preacher. Through exegesis, the text yields certain points, and these points are then modified by the introductory idea.

Consider the following example. A sermon was to be preached on Hebrews 10:26–39.

If we deliberately keep on sinning after we have received the knowledge of the truth, no sacrifice for sins is left, but only a fearful expectation of judgment and of raging fire that will consume the enemies of God. Anyone who rejected the law of Moses died without mercy on the testimony of two or three witnesses. How much more severely do you think a man deserves to be punished who has trampled the Son of God under foot, who has treated as an unholy thing the blood of the covenant that sanctified him, and who has insulted the Spirit of grace? For we know him who said, "It is mine to avenge; I will repay," and again, "The Lord will judge his people." It is a dreadful thing to fall into the hands of the living God.

Remember those earlier days after you had received the light, when you stood your ground in a great contest in the face of suffering. Sometimes you were publicly exposed to insult and persecution; at other times you stood side by side with those who were so treated. You sympathized with those in prison and joyfully accepted the confiscation of your property, because you knew that you yourselves had better and lasting possessions.

So do not throw away your confidence; it will be richly rewarded. You need to persevere so that when you have done the will of God, you will receive what he has promised. For in just a very little while,

> "He who is coming will come and not delay.
> But my righteous one will live by faith.
> And if he shrinks back,
> I will not be pleased with him."

But we are not of those who shrink back and are destroyed, but of those who believe and are saved.

Exegesis of the text led to these results:

1. Verse 39 was considered to be an interpretive key because it identifies two groups of people: those who shrink back and those who believe.

2. The passage was divided in two sections of relatively the same length. Verses 26–31 have to do with the necessity of believing in the Son of God, while verses 32–39 point to the necessity of perseverance on the part of those who do believe.

3. The text then yields two main points for the sermon:
  I. You need to believe.
  II. You need to persevere.

Admittedly other preachers might handle the material differently. For example, the passage could be divided for two sermons instead of one. Even though other exegetical outlines are possible, their number is still limited. When it comes to formulating an introduction, however, the choices are innumerable. It so happens that this particular sermon was written in the late fall when the preacher and just about everyone else had football on the brain. The sermon introduction grew out of a connection between late autumn football fever and the text. The train of thought ran like this:

> Isn't it interesting how televised football games seem to force the viewer to choose sides? Even if you've barely heard of the teams before, watching them for just a few minutes can leave you cheering for one side over the other. Football demands that you take sides, making neutrality virtually impossible. Christianity is a lot like that too. You can either believe and be saved or shrink back and be destroyed.

The essential ingredients for a sermon are now in place. We have a biblical outline and a relevant opener. But we're still not done. The main points have been derived from the Bible (as they must be), but we still need to articulate them in terms appropriate to the introductory idea (in this case, choosing sides in TV football games). We end up changing "You need to believe," to "If you're not on Jesus' side, you need to get on his side." And "You need to persevere," becomes "If you're on Jesus' side, you need to stay on his side."

Keep in mind that the introduction does not determine what the main points will be, but it does greatly affect how they will be described. Here is the completed introduction. (Notice the plural noun *choices* in the structural contact point at the end.)

INTRODUCING THE SERMON

Many people believe that the distinguishing characteristic of the month of December is the Christmas holiday. If you stop and think about it, however, you begin to realize that what is memorable about December is not Christmas as much as football. College football. Pro football. Bowl football. Basketball and hockey are underway, but in December football is in its prime. This is the time of year when we find ourselves watching football on television for the simple reason that there is nothing else on television except a few animated Christmas specials we have already seen nine times. During December you are likely to find yourself watching a game between teams in which you have had absolutely no previous interest—games like Kansas City versus Cincinnati or TCU against SMU. Did you ever notice that as you watch such a game you gradually begin to get involved in it? Even though you have never seen or heard of the teams before, after a few minutes you're cheering for the the guys in the green jerseys. Kids pick this up. When there's a game on TV, the first thing they ask is, "Who are we rooting for?" Football is like that. It makes you choose sides. It calls for commitment. It does not lend itself to neutral observation.

Football is not the only thing in which neutrality is difficult or impossible. Christianity does not lend itself to neutral observation either. Jesus said, "He who is not with me is against me" (Matthew 12:30). Following Jesus is the ultimate issue of life and death in which there can be no neutrality. "I tell you the truth, whoever hears my word and believes him who sent me has eternal life and will not be condemned; he has crossed over from death to life" (John 5:24). The difference between accepting Christ and rejecting him is nothing less than the difference between life and death. The Apostle Paul emphasized the same idea in saying, "You were dead in your transgressions and sins, in which you used to live. . . .But because of his great love for us, God. . .made us alive with Christ." (Ephesians 2:1–4). Hebrews 10 concludes by making the same sharp distinction between "those who shrink back and are destroyed" and those who "believe and are saved" (verse 39). The life-and-death issues addressed by Christianity make neutrality impossible.

Two groups of people are described in Hebrews 10:26–39. One group rejects Christ; the other follows him in spite of difficulty and opposition. Which side are you on? As much as we dislike the idea, when it comes to spiritual life and death, there are but two choices. According to the Bible, you are born again to spiritual life. If you sense that your life is really going nowhere, filled with stress, anxiety, uncertainty, and unhappiness the underlying problem may very well be that you are still on the wrong side spiritually. You need to cross over from death to life. If you have already received Christ and the life he offers, you may still be struggling to live the spiritual life successfully. Hebrews 10:26–39 addresses both needs. The heart of this passage is the simple message that Jesus Christ calls you to follow him. Hebrews 10 summarizes the two choices involved in following Christ.

Although the structural contact point is short and comes at the end of the introduction, it must not be taken for granted. By identifying the main points that are coming, it bridges the gap between introduction and sermon and leads the audience into an encounter with the Word.

Conclusion

No contact, no start. Your precious sermon, reflecting hours of diligent Bible study and careful organization, will evaporate into the rafters of the church building unless its introduction makes contact with the secular world, the Bible, the needs of people, and the main body of the sermon. Don't settle for two or three of these contact points. Go for all four.

For the novice, the process of developing the four contact points of a sermon introduction—not to mention the whole sermon—may seem like a long, complicated, tedious task. Take heart! Experienced preachers can accomplish all the goals of a successful introduction in two or three hours. As a matter of fact, once your mind is trained to think homiletically, it's hard to shut it off!

Here are a final few suggestions for developing better introductions.

1. Read or listen to your recent sermon introductions. Look for the four contact points. You are undoubtedly using one or more of them already. How can they be improved?

85

2. Isolate the contact point that you overlook most frequently or have the most trouble developing. Consciously focus on it over the next few sermons.

3. Have one of the members of your congregation or staff read this book. Ask the person to jot down the four contact points as you preach each message. You will soon learn whether your audience is hearing what you think you're saying.

4. Write out a few introductions word for word. You may not continue this practice, but it won't hurt to try. It will help you greatly in identifying and improving the four contact points.

Notes

Chapter One

1. Frederick Buechner, *Telling the Truth: The Gospel as Tragedy, Comedy, and Fairy Tale* (San Francisco: Harper and Row, 1977), p.23.

2. John Broadus, *On the Preparation and Delivery of Sermons*, rev. J. B. Weatherspoon (New York: Harper and Brothers, 1944), p. 103.

3. Haddon W. Robinson, *Biblical Preaching: The Development and Delivery of Expository Messages* (Grand Rapids: Baker, 1980), p. 167.

4. Broadus, p. 267.

5. John R. W. Stott, *Between Two Worlds: The Art of Preaching in the Twentieth Century* (Grand Rapids: Eerdmans, 1982), p. 244.

6. Broadus, p. 101.

7. James S. Stewart, *Heralds of God* (reprint, Grand Rapids: Baker, 1972), p. 177.

Chapter Two

1. Lloyd M. Perry, *Biblical Sermon Guide* (Grand Rapids: Baker, 1970), pp. 36–37.

2. Garrison Keillor, "Attitude," *New Yorker* 54:28 (August 27, 1979): 34.

Chapter Three

1. Lewis B. Smedes, "Preaching to Ordinary People," *Leadership* 4:4 (Fall 1983): 116.

2. Charles E. Ferrell, "The King Who Commands Peace," *Vital Sermons of the Day* 2:4 (July/August 1984): 3.

3. John Thompson, "Thank God for the Interruptions," *Vital Sermons of the Day* 2:4 (July/August 1984): 6.

4. Lloyd M. Perry, *Biblical Sermon Guide* (Grand Rapids: Baker, 1970), p. 92.

5. *Vital Sermons of the Day*, now defunct, was published by Virgil W. Hensley, Inc., of Tulsa, Oklahoma. The value of *Vital Sermons* was not that it published the polished masterpieces of famous preachers, but that it published what I believe are typical American sermons, the kind preached by thousands of preachers every Sunday. These opening sentences were culled from *Vital Sermons* and the author's own files.

Chapter Four

1. M. T. Billingsley, "Facing Up to Flunking Out," *Vital Sermons of the Day* 2:2 (March/April 1984): 13.

2. Joe A. Harding, "Resurrection Living for a Happier Home," *Vital Sermons of the Day* 2:6 (November/December 1984): 5.

Chapter Five

1. John Knox, *The Integrity of Preaching* (New York: Abingdon, 1947) pp. 26–27.

2. Joe A. Harding, "Resurrection Living for a Happier Home," *Vital Sermons of the Day* 2:6 (November/December 1984): 5.

Chapter Six

1. D. Martin Lloyd-Jones, *Preaching and Preachers* (Grand Rapids: Zondervan, 1971), p. 199.

Notes

Chapter Seven

1. Phillips Brooks, *Lectures on Preaching* (reprint, Grand Rapids: Baker, 1969), p. 209.

Chapter Eight

1. The various preaching textbooks deal with this process at length. In this book I have attempted to develop an approach to sermon introductions that is adaptable to various sermonic processes.

2. Lloyd M. Perry, *Biblical Sermon Guide* (Grand Rapids: Baker, 1970), p. 28.